Praise for the poetry of John Bourne

Whatta sock to the psyche John Bourne's poetry provides. A warm witty love permeates all - from a six-year-old first kiss behind a backyard garage through a wildflower garden of friends, lovers, life moments to the last years with his beloved wife. Always the insightful rebel - "no one in rebellion except me" he says of a childhood classroom - he calls us to live life with raw awareness and to the max - and then poetize it - with a ready twinkle, "and a scar to show a little wear / just to prove that we were there" (from the title poem of this rich collection.)
Lewie Pell, author of *Move Toward Me..., Plenty of Room*, and *Petals of Grace*

I couldn't stop rereading and rereading John Bourne's poems. Enthralled and provoked, I was arguing and singing and crying and having many a cosmic chuckle with him. He sorely and sweetly stirred my own memories and imaginings. What a journey into the mind and life of a sensitive man -- a poet and a philosopher to be sure. Mr. *Homo teaseratus*, indeed. He's written so many *peaches*! If you don't think it's possible to go from a black hole to "a small vanilla ice cream in a paper cup with sprinkles," just watch him. Furthermore, I will never see a hot air balloon rising in the sky without saying a prayer of thanks for my favorite atheist.
Gwynn Popovac, visual artist, author of *Wet Paint*

In one of his best poems--and they're all good--John Setliffe Bourne identities the poet's goal, or perhaps quest is a better word: "To try to make a thing of air that is something more than air." He does it, with strength and humor and even a little bit of sadness. He shows us his soul and, by extension, the soul of the world. When you finish this book you will know that you have been somewhere. And, like Eliot's Magi, you will "no longer be at ease in the old dispensations." For you have seen that rarest of things, something made of air that is more than air. John Bourne is a poet. And something more.
Dan Maguire, author of *Somewhere Between* and *Finding the Words*

TO MAKE A THING OF AIR

Poems

by

John Setliffe Bourne

To Make a Thing of Air

By
John Setliffe Bourne

Visit our website **at www.StillwaterPress.com** for more information.

First Stillwater River Publications Edition
Published in cooperation with Brief Candle Books, Providence, RI
ISBN-10:0-692-29387-6
ISBN-13: 978-0-69229-387-4

Library of Congress Control Number: 2014951835

1 2 3 4 5 6 7 8 9 10
Written by John Setliffe Bourne
Cover Photo: Anonymous
Back Cover Photo: "John Emoting" by Adele M. Bourne
Cover design by Dawn M. Porter
Published by Stillwater River Publications, Glocester, RI, USA

John Setliffe Bourne
April 12, 1933—April 3, 2012

This book is presented as John's memorial as he always preferred to speak for himself.

Acknowledgments

These poems were published in the following publications:

"At the Haiku Convention," *U.S. 1 Worksheets*

"A Thing of Air," *Asheville Poetry Review*

"After Work," S*outhern Poetry Review*

"Butterfly," *Oberon*

"Class Picture," *Mississippi Review*

"Explication," *U.S. 1 Worksheets*

"Finding the Big Dipper," *Mad Poets Review*

"Gardener," *Oberon*

"Jazz Man," *Paterson Literary Review*

"Mending," *Paterson Literary Review*

"My Father," *Pittenbruach Press: A Slice of Apple, a family anthology*

"My Mother," *Pittenbruach Press: A Slice of Apple, a family anthology*

"Peaches" *Paterson Literary Review*

"Pluto," *U.S.1Worksheets*

"Professor Wanted Apples," *U.S 1 Worksheets*

"Poem without a Name," *U.S. 1 Worksheets*

"Searching for Adele," *Mad Poets Review*

"Snow Geese," *Oberon*

"Summer Night by a Pool," *Mad Poets Review*

"The Last Visit," *Paterson Literary Review*

"The Poetry Workshop," *Mad Poets Review*

"Teacher," *Paterson Literary Review*

"Ut Pictura Poesis," *Paterson Literary Review*

"What Have You Done, America?" *Pedestal Magazine*

"What to Pack When You Go to Heaven," *Oberon*

Preface

The poems in *To Make a Thing of Air* are divided into three sections:

Part I—"Poems from a Small Planet" is arranged in more or less biographical order (omitting most of *Love Letters for Everyone but My Wife*, an early collection John later tactfully retitled as *Searching for Adele*).

Part II—"The Professor Who Wanted Apples" includes many of the poems John loved to present at poetry readings. He described them as poems "to amaze your friends, neighbors, and lucky standers-by, suitable for holiday events, family reunions, subway presentations…"

Part III—"A Mind of Winter," gathers poems from 2009 to 2012, composed during John's second and final struggle with cancer, which included two stays in a rehabilitation facility/nursing home and simultaneous out-patient chemotherapy and radiation at Jefferson Hospital in Philadelphia.

John described these experiences as:

…a double whammy, so that I was in various degrees of incapacity much of the time. As a diversion, since I had no interest in reading, or much of the world for that matter, I spent sleepless days and nights reviewing my past—and a lot came bubbling up, asking to be heard.

Some of it is pretty good, some just turned up from the raw edges of memory, so that voices would just start themselves and get written down in a scrawled notebook. Much of the material reflects the anxiety of the moment, as well as disparate thoughts out of the blue, or black, as the case may have been. One voice in particular remains unidentified, a lady who kept saying, "Oh, you're so clever." She sounded nice, young, no doubt pretty, but now just a voice.

Other voices include memories of a failed first marriage, and classmates in rural Oregon. Another curious aspect to the experience was a sudden empathy for all things, for example, looking at the horses

outside my window, a serious concern for how their lives would end,
what unexpected surprise, the soft eyes open and startled, and for the
50,000 or so wounded in our recent misadventures overseas, lying
about in VA hospitals, small homes, often with divorce as a final
reward, the future maimed or crippled beyond repair.

***

John especially wanted to thank our family, and friends, especially Gloria Burton, Lewis and Christiana Pell, Vladimir Popovac and Gwynne Popovac, Dan Maguire, and his doctors, nurses, and therapists. My special thanks to Nancy Scott and Patricia M. Robbins.

Compiling John's poems into this book has been a way to keep his spirit and humor close at hand.

Adele M. Bourne

TABLE OF CONTENTS

PART II: THE PROFESSOR WHO WANTED APPLES

PART III: A MIND OF WINTER

PART I

Poems from a Small Planet

*We are placed on this earth some little time
that we might learn to bear the beams of love.*

William Blake

To Make a Thing of Air

The voice said, *Why do you draw*
these simple lines and to what end?

And I replied—it is the wand
of my disposition from time to time

to try to make a thing of air
that is something more than air,

some merely mortal carving
fabricated out of whimsy,

with no more meaning, you might say,
than a passing cloud on a winter day,

and perhaps dropped in, a jot of thought,
though surely, really, not a lot—

and then a scar to show a little wear
just to prove that we were there.

Class Picture

The school principal, a sheep dog in a blue suit, nips
at the youngsters' heels, pushing them back
into a long, slightly arcing semicircle.

Six rows of children—the first sit on the grass—
the last row (the tallest boys) stand alone,
speculating with each other.

The camera is a tall black box on a ten-foot tripod.
The gray-haired photographer crawls up a ladder,
surveys his view, then descends with a tape
to measure distances for his picture.

Back on his perch, he pulls a black hood over his head,
and says *All right!* (then the sweep of the camera)
all right, don't look around, all right, warns the man,
stay right where you are!

At last the great, black box stops its sweep—the man
emerges from under the hood, and signals his work done.

From where I'm standing, I can just make out distant dots—
now disappearing in the bright afternoon sun—red, blue,
black, orange, more blue? and then, turning to leave,
suddenly I think of the fifth grade—and Charlie Swanson,
who, agile of both mind and body, appeared in *both ends*
of our class picture *forever.*

My Father

My father didn't live on a hill,
was not famous for his generosity,
or his horses,
or even for his garden.

My father didn't run the country
or a corporation
as fathers do.

Or hurl the javelin,
cut down trees,
or fill the banks with dough.

What my father *did* do was—
teach me to spell *obbligato,*
whistle through my teeth,
always dance with one wallflower
at every dance,

and to make a fist.

Jill

You were the first one.
It was the first grade,
and we'd walk home from school
to your house where
I was allowed to watch your mother
braid your long golden hair.

On the front porch, we had the games
all the six-year-olds were playing—
hopscotch chalked on the sidewalk,
and slippery jacks, at which you excelled,
I remaining stuck forever at *threesies.*

We played doctor. Unencumbered by prurient
notions of any merit, we failed to progress
beyond pink candy pills and fake stethoscope.

Once, you took me by the hand,
led me back behind your garage,
between two narrow walls,
excitement in your eyes.

Pumped up—with a rush not to get caught,
you put your arms around me
in a determined clinch. I can still feel your kiss—
a hurried dry arrangement.

Later, you instructed me not to walk home
with that other girl—the one who walked about
brazenly, her arm around the other boys.

So I tried that, of course...
and found it *very much to my liking*!
And so began my long apprenticeship in
disobedience.

6

Matinee

Jean Arthur, in her smart, tight
cowgirl outfit, is standing
on the motion picture ranch lot,

and discomfited, Joel McCrea is
abashed at "all that female equipment,"
and he was right: buttons, clasps,

mysterious bones to push things up,
and there he was, just a cowpoke,
wearing studio chaps and spurs,

fake guns—figuring the odds,
yes, abashed, that was his style,
a really nice fellow.

Of course, it was all so predictable,
a story that could just write itself,
like *all* those stories that made us

exchange our time and money
for something else—a better story
than we could possibly have,

at least then, surrounded by
other noisy kids, popcorn on the floor,
gum under every seat.

My Mother

My mother was a hard case—if she's in Heaven
right now, she has it redecorated to suit her taste,
and will move on to redoing that "other place" next.

When she entered a room, she'd take in the layout,
the range of colors, the patterns and angles, seeing
how things fit together—wherever she looked she saw
possibilities—in rooms, in houses, above all in *people*.

Then would come the solutions, uninvited, pointed,
sometimes on the mark, perhaps, but still—
not everyone is ready for a complete makeover.

Sadly, she's gone now, but thought to leave me here
to continue her good work—the thankless, unending
task of setting things right, the proper balance.

Now, about that so-called life of yours,
I have a few suggestions....

How to Better Express Yourself

Where do you stand on the matter of split infinitives?

To narrowly split an infinitive is bad form according to one school,
now dead I would hope, that place where I struggled to make
the grades where Rice Penmanship called for a concrete arm moved
enmasse to make a thousand slanted lines and curlicues
as in /////////// and *0000000.*

Yes, those were the days, we sat straight up, no one in rebellion
except me against the boring lockstep teaching, the certitude
of the ancient principal, Miss White, who suspected me of the graffiti
in the halls and bathrooms, of besmirching her high station and of
being girl crazy, but I loved only one girl, Bonnie, who would wink at
me when I said something funny to share with the other inmates, boys
and girls condemned to never split anything except maybe a Baby
Ruth or U-No Bar, but not a hair there in rural Oregon, where the kids
said I was too "citified" and so unlikely to ever live the good life.

There were no cows or horses in our own backyard though we had a
few chickens with names like Nelly Bly and Felicia who spoke their
own language and never accused me of anything untoward, and I just
wanted to gently make this observation from long ago and I wonder
whatever happened to Bonnie, her indelible winks, her wonderful blue
eyes.

Uncle Jack

She was my mother's little sister,
Aunt Kathryn, a tall, shapely, witty brunette—
dead ringer for Barbara Stanwyck—and
occasional clerk typist for a bumptious nephew—
always good for a ride to the park,
a sardonic joke.

She and my mother called each other "dearie,"
and the natural order of things was that
she would be unmarried forever and ever,
or so it seemed....

Then one day, a man showed up,
also tall and lean, who eventually became
                              Uncle Jack.

In the evening, they'd walk about the neighborhood,
talking softly, a gentle promenade
drifting under suburban trees.

One night, returning home,
I saw them together—there,
through the living room window.

He was holding her, kissing her,
his hands moving across her back,
caressing with firm, tremulous fingers,
searching for his children.

Boston: U.S. Coast Guard

Stationed in Boston, no practical place to go,
the solitary signs of local bars proclaimed their
welcome through the dirty snow—*Schlitz,*
"the beer that made Milwaukee famous,"
and that ubiquitous blue bell of happiness,
Pabst Blue Ribbon Beer.

Once inside, past the shuffleboard and the juke box,
across the dirty, creaking floor, there—
over the dark wooden bar with the beef jerky
and pickled eggs, would be the best image of all—

a blue and silver lake that shimmered endlessly—
and sitting in this magical lake,
an American Indian in a birch bark canoe
hawked the white man's firewater—
Hamm's Beer! ("It's the water!")

And then, for a dollar,
you were home again,
or at least in the neighborhood.

Finding the Big Dipper

Morgan roadster, Carole Lombard look-a-like,
stars like gangbusters—

Emerging from dinner at an inn high in the hills
of Topanga Canyon, my date exclaimed,
Oh, look, there's the Milky Way!

*Nay, madam, 'tis but a white smudge on the vault
of the heaven,* I gibed.

No, it's the Milky Way. Look at it!

She was tall, and were she mine already, perhaps
she would have coiled about me closer, snakelike,
as we stared up into the night.

As it was, we did a sort of silent dance, our arms
forming an axle about which we wheeled, hands
held tightly, excitingly close in this new relationship.

And there's the Big Dipper. But it's in the wrong place.

But no, I said again, *It's just right. If its handle will tip
down a little more, it will make a question mark.*

It should be over there, she said, with sober rectitude.

But a question mark, I insisted, *standing on the horizon—
the universe questioning itself—is that not fitting?*

Later, she left me for her psychiatrist.

Anecdote of a Marriage

Inge looked to the sky as we dropped bombs on her native Dresden,
raped by Russians, she said, or was it American soldiers, all mixed-up,
next, a war bride to an American sergeant, then off to California
where handsome men became husbands—I made number four,
should have checked the merchandise more carefully—inclined
to beer for breakfast, stronger stuff some evenings, but so beautiful,
with golden tresses, a rich laugh, a painter with a discerning eye,
actress, too—in the movies, but never made it big, as they say.

At first, rushing in, I thought I had to bite the apple clear through,
certain this was it, tie up the deal with the right paper work—
marriage—the best there is, isn't it? Then stuck it out as long
as I thought reasonable but it went beyond that the night she pulled
the gun, the disappearing acts, each day a new surprise—
some beyond unpleasant—so I gave the requisite two weeks' notice
and left by the same road I had come by.

And regrets? No, not regret exactly, no time for that, only time enough
to save myself, to trust the steel bars of resolution that had to be forged
and adhered to—in spite of the possibility of a mistake, in spite of
premonitions of the unforgettable later in this collapsing marriage, of
something that could never be recovered.

Short of the Indian funeral pyre, here in America we divide the silver,
the house, even the kids, and then live with the memories—the pictures
of glory at Easter, the bitter cries at Christmas—how easy it is to
damage the only person in your life—the whole damned thing.

Ilka

Oh, you beast! she would say, when I said or did something outlandish
or vulgar—and one night, *John, do you know what you're saying?*
And truth is I was on top of her and had no idea what I was saying
and also no idea I had no idea what I was saying, just a little while
after abandoning my first wife, and there I was hemorrhaging wrong
ideas to my good friend, the lovely Ilka, confused about what to be
attached to, blind with the wine, reaching out in a spare, one-bedroom
apartment—portraits, paintings on the floor—but facing the wall,
my lost artist wife not allowed to mock me or reproach me or add
to the emptiness—and everything pushed up that night, churning
too fast—a lost window now closed tight, the thrash of being
on a strange bed, uncertain in this surround, so unlikely, familiar
but out of joint—the rented couch, the bare walls with their strange
colors—pale yellow, off-white—the Formica coffee table, souvenir
ashtrays.

The Last Visit in New Hope, PA,
which Had Its Own Tiny Railroad

It was easy for her,
she had closed the valves
of her attention like stone,
and she sat, thumbing a book,
still wearing overcoat, gloves,
hat clamped to her head.

What was she dressed against—
the chill she brought into the room?

Stiffening in her straight-backed chair,
three times she announced her departure,
three times I crossed the room
to fill her glass, attempt to stay
her forward motion,
some slight delay—
but she

with single-minded skill,
wove a pattern of farewell,
closing all the doors,
sealing all the exits,
erasing any future,

until at last,
seeing a clear path,
with all the signals set in place,
she went out the door,
just like the New Hope locomotive,
straight down the rail, on time,
with a full head of steam,
and
            no regrets   visible.

Explication

for Vladimir

How could he not understand my poem?
Listen, I explained: the black is for certainty,
the green is for uncertainty,
the red is for passion—
and the yellow—well,
everyone knows about yellow.

The purple is for all the strength I could muster—
and there—near the bottom—
the gray streaked with orange,
that's the ending
as well as I could write it,
the *denouement*, if you will.

The couplet is, I admit, a bit obscure—
but as for the rest, well, now you know!

Ut Pictura Poesis

Ut Pictura Poesis—
a poem should be like a picture,
an old canon, and hard to achieve,
but consider these:

A man and a woman moving toward each other
on a dusk-colored bed of lawn. They meet,
objects fall to the ground, they embrace,
then flutter downward, an unspeaking heap.

Except for the colors—and that there are
two people instead of one—I can imagine
Duchamp's *Nude Descending,* or the fine
terraces of Japanese gardens spiraling to earth.

Or sea creatures, churning at the bottom
of a green sea, caught in life's pattern,
blind to their enemies.

Ganja

It was the *ganja*,
she said, and
(I would add) the absence of a censoring
eye, as well as the accident of distance,
and, oh well, the unexpected:
O*P*P*O*R*T*U*N*I*T*Y

Yes, the *ganja*,
which provides its own license,
its own easy way to
freedom....

Or the excitement of discovery,
perhaps—
a hero from some brimming place,
where there are others who exclaim
fastidious glory.

And, after all,
how much can we expect
(can one expect?)
from these terribly mortal millions,

these all-too-human creatures,
when churned with drugs,
moonlight-crafted promises,
and especially the too seldom
ecstasy.

Summer Night by a Pool

Feeling like a character in a Fitzgerald novel,
or one of those musicals where they wear
blazers and straw hats, I followed you down
to the pool—to the boat house—where
your husband would never find us—
or whoever it was should never know.

The key was missing, so we camped
on the narrow porch with your fine,
narrow head dangerously close
to an enormous pipe wrench, old tools.

It *was* like a play, you know—oh, not fiction,
but the movement of people in life's opaque
little drama, where we are constantly hoping
for happier endings.

And then, in the stillness,
it became so smooth,
like silver fish dancing in the moon,
and I was only afraid of the noise.

Searching for Adele

The first music was the ocean,
        followed by
                rivers and trees—

scatterings of birds,
        great commotions of creatures
            rushing on

in the gusty roar of life,
        death—collisions
            great and small—

and then, through time—
        a calming,
            and a new music—

your voice, discovered
        in a barren field—
            singing the song of you.

Bower Bird

Do you know the Bower Bird?

It builds a nest to pass a test,
a matter of taste, entire.

The lady bird will assess the nest, look for the best
to meet her critic's eye, I don't know why—but
there's this test—pebbles and twigs, a bower of flowers,
all meant to please…arrest.

And when she chooses, thus, the die is cast, at last—
no turning back—this harmony of bush and rock,
this trial of nerve and verve, this beginning and
beginning and beginning.

Tell a Lie, Save a Life

Some say now that it was a *civil war*, there in far-off Korea,
their north against *their* south, and *we* were going to war,
though not called a war—there in this age of euphemism,
simply a "police action."

Anyway, there was a big net to catch would-be warriors,
it was the draft, coming right at me like a big fat wave,
so I found shelter in the U.S. Coast Guard Reserve.

Months after being accepted in the Guard, there was
a second fitness test, the last before being shipped off
to San Francisco along with the other "boots." If I failed
for any reason, I would go into the army, the draft, join
my classmates, learn to shoot straight, maybe get killed.

The doctor—I suppose he was a doctor—tested blood pressure,
looked at my teeth—no more than three cavities allowed—
and for a final bump, held his wristwatch to my ear.

"Hear that?" he asked.
I didn't hear a thing, but, what's the chance he's wearing a watch
that's not running? So I said, "Sure."

Once in the Guard, which I envisioned as pretty girls and
the beach in San Diego, I found that the landing barges
on D-Day were manned by *us*! a specialty for which I would be
well-qualified, should it come to that.

But let me tell you about something else. Once upon a time,
playing Real Estate, we sat around a big table: me, my new
wife, two hungry salesmen, one anxious house seller, and lots
of legal paper. I was the star signer, the big enchilada
in this whole hoo-haw.

At the bottom of a jumble of legal scripture, there was one final question: "Have you ever gone through bankruptcy?"
So, what were the chances? I was in New Jersey, three thousand miles from home, buying a hundred-year-old house on a shady street in a smart little town—there almost forty years now.

So I said "No," and that was a lie, and that's the truth!

Four Lane Road

after a painting by Edward Hopper

What does the lady want, leaning out the window
of the white frame building? What is she saying—
so urgent that needs attention *now*, probably
should have been attended to before?

Most likely something he's been avoiding here
where lack of motion is the norm. He'll have to get up
off that fragile chair and get moving,
perhaps douse the cigar, anyway, get it done.

The Brown Suit

It was important, the brown suit with wide lapels,
so I could blend in—be like everyone else,
there in the villages—not be stoned
for some act of difference.

It was a change in style, how things were done—
were to be done—in the executive suites,
the walnut walls, the rows of names in gold and bronze.

And so I endured, prospered even, always on time,
carried by trains, buses, airplanes, to all those faces
with their shields of approval, the doors open,
hands shaken, and the agreements—
all kinds of agreements.

Disorder

I sit in my car, start the engine,
then stop to think—

Yes, it's just as if it makes sense,
and here I go again, one more time,
acting as if the manicured streets,
the orderly banks, our cities—the whole
unlikely arrangement makes any sense,
could, in any way, be deciphered....

I think of my old drinking pal—Roger,
one night, a few drinks, and I got serious—
played devil's advocate, *What's it all about,
Roger*, I chided, *what's with this mysterious
universe of ours, any clues?*

Surprising me, he became upset,
his face flushed—some nerve struck,
I guess—he threw his glasses to the floor saying,
*It makes no sense to me either,
I never could make it out!*

I remember, so long ago, my grandfather,
a precision engineer, threw *his* glasses
into the fireplace, cracking the lenses,
the gold rims bent, lying in the ashes
on the cold gray stone.

Not resentment at the lost gods, I think,
but some streak of anger, something that
had to break through—perhaps it was just
the long weeks of rain, the floods and the people
in boats—disorder everywhere.

Poem without a Name

When there's a dead child in the room,
one must avoid…certain details.

Confine yourself to the weather,
the cost of coal—anything full of innocence.

Do not think of dark oak,
smooth velvet, polished brass.

Be as thoughtful as carved granite or marble
standing in a wild field.

Pluto

Pluto, they're beginning to talk about you,
something about losing your status as the planet farthest
from our reluctant mother the sun.

After all those solitary years aloft, your reputation
in all the books, nudged aside by some big glob of ice—
so far away, where darkness is the only rule.

And who are *we* to pronounce your place in the cosmos,
even though each of us is, in the smallest way,
a dying star, far from everything we know.

Hunting in a Northern Clime

Just escaped from the cold, moving briskly
into the kitchen, I attempt to press an icy hand
to my wife's cheek or under her silk blouse,

but she shrinks back with a yelp,
unwilling to share her private warmth
or yield to this silly business, so I give up,

trek back outside where hamburger patties,
frozen peas, and Arnold's Whole Wheat bread
wait in the car. Overhead, the local stars look down,

those ancient forms—Orion with his
mammoth bow stalking the elusive Taurus,
while his companion *canis major* chases a rabbit,

And I think of another time—half an ice age ago, when
Morrie (the Strong) would come in from the icy hills
after a hard day, chasing the local *plat du jour*—

a big wiggly eel, say, or lovely hunk of walrus—
and walk into the warmth of his cave, near the small fire,
and hold up his hands to the lovely Loreena (the Soft),

not just to tease, but to celebrate the safe return of the great
hunter, *homo teaseratus*, in from the terrible cold, eager to share
with his beloved some slight token, some quick surprise!

Teacher

It's Room 104 in the Allentown Public School,
and she stands alone in the large classroom,
windows open to the welcome spring weather.

All about her, the wreckage of another school year—
piles of books, unfinished student projects,
a rebellion of scattered desks abandoned by
their small occupants and now a part
of the big job ahead—cleaning out cupboards,
storing things in boxes, taking down all those
posters with their entreaties for peace and tolerance.

High on a wall, the alphabet parades its stuff—A B C D—
perennial challenge to that steady stream of young
minds, and below this, a string of her favorite quotes
from Franklin to Einstein to Desmond Tutu.

The road traveled once again—over the bumps
and obstacles, the petty dictates from administration,
the struggle to maintain programs with shrinking budgets,
outsiders who tried to interfere, the hard-won, small victories,
and at the end, always this mess.

The teacher sat down on one of the old, well-used chairs,
and thought about the final student fair, the long line
of students who would be gone forever—and then,
for just a moment, had this thought:

wouldn't it be nice if suddenly a crowd would come
cheering noisily up the hall carrying a huge, chocolate
sundae under a mountain of whipped cream, topped
with a big maraschino cherry—just for her!

But no, only the silence of the empty room—and then another thought, drifting over the loss of ice cream—that because of her, some students will go on to see and do things with a little more clarity, perhaps, or ability or strength. And that was sweet, too.

Charles Simic

When making poems,
I sometimes add meanings
to my meaning

but he to tell of fish
brings out the trout
on a bare platter

a bone here
a bone there

the flat moist eye
the pattern of water
beneath our feet

how things fit together
the river of our concern.

In Storage

We were on the outskirts of Boston, Cambridge,
on a residential street, crossing routes—

managing a fitful exchange between spouses, moving
children from his and hers back to us and ours,

and in the attendant waxing and waning of too many husbands,
ex-wives, nervous rejoinders, you called me "Rodney!"

And then we continued our separate ways, and I thought about
the strange way the mind stores ideas—names—in compartments,

because there are times when, in anger or exasperation—
some helpless, thoughtless moment—there comes to me

the name of my first wife, that dead stranger,
so quick to the fore—not Mary or Karen—none of those,

but apparently from that one place where wives and husbands
are stored, stuck together, just waiting to be called

in those special moments of need or dread, a reminder,
perhaps, of how the remnants of love hang about,

ready to emerge in times of confusion or stress, reaching
into our lives at any moment—unexpected, unwelcome, real.

An Evening with Billy Collins

The last time I saw Billy Collins
there were hundreds of us—
and he was just this tall
(see my thumb and forefinger?),
a small figure, looking just like his picture,
bald, jovial—just plain him,

and he had our absolute attention,
not looking for something new,
I suspect—though possibly—
but more to hear a favorite song again,
to be rubbed once more where
it counts for so much…

just Mr. Collins, half a mile away
in a large auditorium, rolling it out,
all that good stuff we came for,
will keep coming for as long as
there are auditoriums to hold us,
Billy to care about us.

True Pictures

The dead speak twice.
Their ghosts run along our bones,
smiling their dead smiles.

Sometimes the way he laughed,
head held high in a great, snorting bray,

or, one afternoon, famished for attention,
the way the blemish on her lip quivered.

To imagine these in a rough, sodden place—
no, the image is false, impossible.

The true picture is at the corner of the eye
darting in—hand with a gun, fist
full of pills, hopes strangling.

Doctor Freud

Dr. Freud teaches us that all is not well in the clear landscape of the mind, that tricky rivulets can run deep, skirmishing with the simplicities, such as forgotten memories of friends and events.

He teaches us fear of going through a long tunnel may come from hidden streams—from memories of giants with hammers breaking dishes, breaking down doors, charging each other with fists and words.

Teaches us to reconsider the tools of excavation—not to rely on bridges that span the canyons of avoidance—not to tamp down ghosts of the past—mothers and fathers in turmoil, pushing through it all.

Old Lovers

Old lovers have voices too, only not so loud,
not so clear—like Madeleine, who says repeatedly—
Well, my dear, you have competition now.

That phone call, that was the end of that, but then
it doesn't end—won't end—since day or night, unbidden,
it's just one of the many calls the brain makes…
and you're always home.

Old lovers, those long almost forgotten loves—
they have their way with you—even after everything
to be said has been said, finally said—then they keep on
saying it again—Madeleine with the taunt, the sudden
announcement, the surprise….over.

And old lovers bring their pictures, memory's photographs—
some lovely, some not so lovely—that act of meanness
while caught in some turmoil—those words
that can never be undone or withdrawn, and above all—
that first sighting, that first touch—*electric.*

Oh, I tell you, that *we'll always have Paris stuff* is both a joy
and a burden, so insistent, always butting in, as it will,
Yvonne and her provocative *I like for you to touch me…*
a sweet memory, but, then, just an old fact…tired…a statistic.

And so these past lovers keep pestering us, lurking there
on the back porch of memory, whistling idly while we go about
our work or toss about on troubled nights, and who was it
that said one night under emerald willows, a pale yellow sky—
who was it said *forever*?

Snow Geese

When snow geese must fill the sky,
driven to some distant calling,

is this their victory over a tumbling world,
this rush to flight in the free night air

or are they but slaves to cold necessity,
the meanest kind of freedom?

Gardener

Late in the afternoon he comes to do the lawn,
a large presence commanding
a caravan of machines—

a big red mower he can ride on,
with a multitude of blades—cut and mulch—
slick as a knife through butter.

You can see he likes the mower
and the ride, so much better than
the old push pull days—

and motorized clippers to reach high bushes,
chunka chunka chunka, brrr brrr brrr-rrmnt!
Two hours in the hot New Jersey sun,

then it's time for a break—we take two chairs
under a garden umbrella on the newly-trimmed lawn,
and have soft drinks, one for him, one for me.

His first drink down all-at-once, and a second to savor
later, he's all sweat and soil with one more job to go,
and we discuss some of the currents in his life right now—

medium news here, job OK, wife not too unhappy,
although this week she has an attitude—the other,
older stuff I already know about and leave alone.

Fifty dollars on printed paper I hand him,
not a lot for two cokes and a little conversation,
this little chunk of crumpled paper—

and then he's off in his truck to earn more printed paper—
some for the doctor, some for his autistic son,
some for his ex-wife.

Lorna
(*nee Ingeborg Charlotte Düssler-Düring, 1926-96)*

These words demand an image—
a rush of golden hair
framed about a lovely face,
all bright future, photographed
beside a summer tree,
a small ribbon completing the effect.

Lorna, not her given name, rather,
invented for show business,
for beguilement, a mask, perhaps
a spider's trick—anyway,

a pose, machinery for show—
jugglers and clowns on stilts,
the lady in pink tights,
the shiny tiara made of glass.

Not *my* Lorna, not now, simply Lorna,
a poem—another use for a dead wife,
the theatre dark and empty,
the lights out—
everyone gone home.

Waterfall

The rumble of a waterfall
begins its rush on mountain top
where tiny streams and narrow brooks
begin to fall their distant way.

From cloud, from rain, from hidden well,
all saunter downward falling free,
past scattered rocks and twisted trees
that form a pattern, curve and bend.

No one is there to sense the breeze,
the rush of water crashing by,
the crackle of a breaking limb
that slips into the foaming stream.

The surging water keeps it course,
cascading to the journey's end,
its final moments in a rush
as ruffling sound and vision blend.

The Man Who Married a Woman Who Didn't
Have a Complaint Window

The man said to his wife, "Where are the sardines,
I have looked high and low and there is no sign
of that lowly fish, the sardine, not hide nor hair."

The woman stopped mopping the floor to say,
"How should I know where everything is,
go look for yourself," but the man said,
"I have been looking for hours,
and there is no fish, nary a fish can I find—
and so I'd like to file a complaint."

At these words the lady stopped mopping,
turned, and shook her mop vigorously, explaining:
"Well! There's no complaint window 'round here,
and I don't want to hear any more about it!"

Nonplussed, the man mused…is it possible
I married a woman without a complaint window?
First thing I did (oh, so long ago) was examine her—
teeth OK, two breasts, belly button—and toes, plenty
of toes, a good ten or twenty, I'm sure. But I didn't look
for a complaint window, or a Help Desk, some sympathetic
quarter where help might come happily and readily.

He tried again: "Mrs. Wife, light of my life, fire of my loins,
great spirit who shares my every thought, I need sardines,
and have no interest in the proprieties, that is, the fine points—
and this is my complaint: *I am sardine-less!*"

"And you, my industrious mate, you move things around,
hide them. I will not even discuss my lost Hawaiian shirts,
or neckties with the surfing bikini girls…just sardines,
my sole and lowly need, sardines, and you say…."

"I say I have plenty to do besides picking up your things
all the time, and anyway, a cheese sandwich is always nice.
Why not have a nice, warm, melty cheese sandwich.
Maybe later the complaint department will open up,
the complaint lady will come in, and help you with your
fish problem. But I tell you, right now, the complaint department
is closed, and any sardines are up to you."

Then came that silence known between married couples as
the-great-frigid-nobody-better-say-anything-more-for-now silence
and, at last, the man said, "Do you suppose you could help me
find the Velveeta?"

What Have You Done, America?

All those soldiers, stuck in their skin, stuck in hospitals,
languishing in the deep silence.

And the men and women in fractured homes,
their futures dismantled, diminished, curtailed.

What have you done, America?

What have you done to the soul of America?

And all those strangers in strange lands—so many
dead, dying, still to die, and more, still more?

What have you done?

And what have you done, people,
you people—what have you done?

And where is your heart now, America,
your soul punctured, damaged, ravaged.

What have you done, America?

What have you done?

The Trains

In the lands of Goethe and Rilke,
the trains were running on time,
over time, and filled with
human cargo, too terrible
to talk about or write about—
human cargo shipped by train,
too awful to discuss, in the lands
of Goethe and Rilke and that

famous professor, Immanuel Kant,
who was never late, as punctual
as any German can be.
It was said neighbors would set
their watches when he walked by
contemplating the meaning of
moral necessity, the citadels
of pure reason.

Washing my Hands on a Sunday Morning

In the right place my hands are claws to grab
the branches of high trees, grasp creatures of field
and swamp, each day in its rough pattern—

yes, I speak of birds and beasts singing in the wilderness—
but the wild is estranged today—feathers all-a-ruffle,
my bird's eye fixed on other improbables—

skyscrapers and bombs—
men with their claws ready, striving through their days
and nights to build dark futures.

When to Cry

When to cry is when the tears are loaded up—
and they come by the bucket.

Or express train, whatever.

The first time I really cried as an adult was when I was
with my first wife, a World War II war bride.

I said *I tried so hard I just tried so hard* and alarmed,
concerned, she crossed the room, came to me,
caressed and consoled me.

But it was impossible.

And the next time—Kate gone, the florist parked
across the street, approaching our house,
bringing gifts too terrible to receive.

Basketball at the "Y"

It appears to be a family: a fortyish, dark-skinned, mustachioed
father, two boys about eight—and mom, old fashioned, heart-shaped
glasses, pale white skin against a gray sweatshirt.

Whenever the ball flies loose, mom grabs it, won't let go,
stands uncertain in a half crouch, determined to get it going—
but the ball flies out of her hands, over and over.

Too far from the basket to shoot while small hands pester her,
the problem is how to get from here to there—that elusive basket,
so far away, but she's got that ball, fends off the boys—then,

a wild throw. The husband (bemused) watches all this patiently,
the wife hustling the ball, the children scrambling to take it away,
this snapshot of a family at play, but it looks like the kids

will just have to wait until mom learns how to dribble, or decides
to share the ball like a good mom should, or, failing that, until they
all get a little older, including these pups…these baby tigers.

Big Poetry Contest Debate and Intra-Family Duel
or This House isn't Big Enough for the Two of Us!

So it's settled, he said, we duel at dawn, *my* poems against *your* poems.
Okay, she said, my good stuff against your junk!

I am offering you a choice of weapons, *naturellement*—
villanelles, haiku—what have you? Petrarchan sonnets, she said,

blowing a wisp of hair from her lovely forehead, and you can expect
no mercy from me, you bumptious versifier, you

blowhard of the pompous poem. And *I*, said the grand poet,
will scuttle your pathetic little ship of words with language

to rival the sweetest melodies of the sweetest angels in heaven!
Speaking of pathetic, said the lovely lady, my pathetic fallacy

will sink your dumb couplets in a trice, you will never know
what hit you. Oh, yeah, said the handsome poet, swelling

his manly chest and fluffing his thick blond hair, oh yeah,
just you wait 'til my iambs are running circles around your

puny spondees…..*you'll* see! But lo, it came to pass that
Calliope, the muse of poetry, heard all this silly boasting,

which was keeping her from an important nap, and so—
looking down on this contentious pair—took away all their

alleged talent, just like that: *Shish, bang, boom*! One-two-three!
Suddenly the grand poet couldn't rhyme any more—easy stuff

like dapple of the apple, *gone*! And the lovely lady poet couldn't
think of grand themes like the importance of rain and soap.

And now they have nothing to argue about. The grand poet has
taken up restoring old bicycles, and the pretty lady poet keeps

entering chili bake-offs, and nobody knows if they are *more*
happy now, or *less* happy, but we do know Calliope is happy

and grateful because she is getting much needed sleep,
and that is the story of the poetry duel between these two

so-so poets in a so-so time in a so-so place, so there!

Starter Sentences

A starter sentence could be—
I just want to tell you about something
that happened once,
or isn't that a divine sunset,
or even waterfall.

But you never know how it might come out,
like I just want to tell you
you mean the whole world to me,
everything—or even
I just want to die,
which is what my mother said
when the truck with the red lights came
to our house and I was five years-old.

She said one of the kids must have
turned on the gas accidentally
but that wasn't true and
I just want to be clear about this.
One little thing from long ago,
it was so long ago.

Shepherd

I am my father's shepherd. In his wheelchair, I lead him
past strange buildings, through forgotten neighborhoods.

Now beyond the pale of his remembrance, he asks,
where are we, what place is this?

I am my father's father, a role as old as fathers,
as old as sons, and time unravels—and the mystery

only deepens as we come to the end of each other,
the end of the ability to ask, what is this, why?

California Dreaming

What's to be done with these husbands and wives,
now separated after years of making things go,
accustomed to a lifetime richly shared?

How shall *we* fill our nights when conversation
must be pulled from the cold night air,
a photograph at the head of the stair—

And what of that old man down the street,
unkempt, desperate for a bit of conversation—
the aroma of a woman's hair?

Composition

Except that we could not be together in the same room without some
quarrel—the push and shove of old disappointments,

I suppose—the kindness and fondness for my mother, and yes,
love remains, or perhaps only now can return, to contemplate,

to celebrate, in some quiet way, my good fortune, the shape
that I became, scattered and proud, unfocused and focused—

sentimental and angry—and happy to add, my father, that wily
old writer and wit—pleased, too, with an even view of the greater

host, mother earth, the small and the large, the nest, the beginning—
all those flights, the amazing view.

Some Remarks Concerning that Old Gypsy Called Time

I walk about and see the stuff of poetry
everywhere, in the books and magazines
scattered about, in the daily commerce
of our lives.

Hours, days, minutes, years have
been stolen for children, friends, work.

And still things go undone, and above
all, that other business—
those unborn poems.

To what purpose shall we live?
What will be the mark?

It is time to sing of arms and men,
to sling the gaudy javelins of poetry,
to quicken the appetite
for unending failure.

Now that the earth is settling
I need your eyes.

PART II

THE PROFESSOR WHO WANTED APPLES

*"...not in Spanish, not in Greek, not in Latin, not in shorthand,
but in plain American which cats and dogs can understand!"*

Marianne Moore

The Professor Who Wanted Apples

Apples, the man said. Bring me apples.
So they went away and came back a week
later. But when it got down to it, the man
said, these are not apples. These are oranges.

Look: no stem on top, no seeds at the core,
and see: scrape them, off comes this orange fluff.
No, these are oranges.
I want apples.

So they went away and came back again,
and everyone hoped there would be apples.
The many boxes were opened, but soon they
could see: Oranges. Just oranges.

The man was nice about it. It is not easy
to bring apples he said. In a world full of
orange groves, one does not stumble across
large numbers of apples. But try again.

So it was that sometimes there would be a few
apples, but mostly oranges. And the man said it was OK,
they should not give up, but continue to look.
After all, he said, apples don't grow on trees.

Hold This

At the center of truth
is a crack in a star,
laughter emerges from there.

Peaches

after "Peaches" by Gerald Stern

I was eating peaches
and I thought these peaches are
so good they are better than sex,
then I remembered it was Garrison Keillor
who had a long bit about corn, not peaches,
but sweet corn that was better than sex—
he did go on that way,
the whole country listening—
then you have to wonder just what kind
of sex he's getting—
and I thought about the Chinese *yu*—
a red-cheeked peach that cannot aid the dead,
but eaten in time prevents death—
and maybe peaches *are* better than sex,
or maybe nothing is better than sex
it's just that most people think
nothing is better than sex don't they?
But, oh, those peaches were good.

60

After Hours at the Met

It's not easy being a painting in a museum,
standing around all day with a bloody sword
in your hand, furious horses bearing down on you,
and yourself busy raping a bunch of Sabines.

Hard, too, for the ladies, their garments ripped up,
their breasts hanging out every which way, vulnerable
to all kinds of happenstance—a knight's lance gone astray,
eagles dashing about, everywhere mayhem.

And how about posing forever in the damn blue suit,
required to be, oh so perfect, never allowed
to go out and play with the other kids,
climb trees, get good and muddy.

But there's a big change once the lights are out,
the doors bolted, the sleepy guards trundled off to home,
and the paintings left at last alone—
that's when things begin to stir!

The naked lady at the picnic, for example, covers up—oh,
not so quickly, after all these years, but still feels the need
to cloak her nakedness, what with the men just lounging there,
so smug in their smart nineteenth-century suits.

In the next room, Rembrandt, weary of being stared at
by endless spectators, climbs down from his heavy gilt frame
and finds his way down the hall to his favorite tavern,
the one where his credit is still good.

And Leda and the swan, exhausted after hours of foreplay,
knock off for the night—the swan swinging his huge white wings
in a lazy arc, sinks down at the back of the picture, while Leda
settles in the foreground, both grateful for the rest.

Demosthenes on the Beach Practicing
His Oratory Skills

Athens, circa 315 BC

(first, with the pebbles)

The remble izy smebble astaze menlly inda paillin....

The remblz in sha membble ina taze nomemblly indz pailnz....

The remblz inner blemble atstz somblemly indoz pailinz....

The raamle onda beezen heim stet indersomple nicht der playa....

The romble under bezund splain ona plain serengiitiee naya....

The reain in da assanaya memble setenlamely ina palaninnnnn....

(now, without the pebbles)

The rain in Spain....

Fidelity

(*a cautionary poem*)

Be careful what you wish for especially if it involves undressing
a lady called Samantha who lives down the street with a small white
dog named Charlie and a large husband named Brutus
The Bad who drives an eighteen-wheeler truck cross-country
and who likes to shoot things with a double-barreled shotgun
and is sometimes gone for days at a time

and she has been known to come to your house on occasion
just to borrow a cup of this or that—or maybe just tea and sympathy—
and your wife is at Mr. Curlie's having her hair
dyed, and the cat is in the backyard resting or possibly up to

no good, but, be careful when just the right things seem
to come together, and the right door magically opens for just
a moment—because they could actually turn out to be *wrong* things
that will turn the tables—

and we must remember—*one* remembers—how big Brutus
The Terrible is, how your wife will look better in a short
while, how the cat seems able to stay out of trouble after some
disastrous experiences, and that in some neighborhoods that
is plenty—or at least enough—to wish for, even on a hot
August day, or, anytime really, you know, in the mating season.

Hello Out There

Planets "d" and "e" recently spied may be the right size,
in the right place…—Philadelphia Inquirer, 4/22/09

Oh, hi! You don't know me, but I'm saying hello anyway and thinking of you from time to time. Today's paper says there are most likely people or beings or some kind of LIFE out there which is, of course, so provocative, just sizzles the imagination especially the idea of two "earth size planets" recently found hanging round a dim red star 21 light-years away in what they say is a "habitable zone" which might possibly place it a notch or two above Newark, New Jersey, which is close to where I live, about 30 not-so-light minutes away inhabited by people or beings much like me, or LIFE you could call it, and I live on West 3rd St. The astronomers found you by the "characteristic wobble" of one or more of your neighbor stars that have a working gravitational relationship with your planet and this discovery provoked excitement, too, about a so-called innermost planet "e" which has a year of just 66 days, so things happen a lot faster there, I mean Christmas every 66 days, imagine the cost, and my name is John, in case you figure a way to say hello back, and I live, as I said, on West 3rd St. next to the old McClain House, which they don't live in anymore but a new family who goes by the name McDonald, or perhaps Maguire. And the article also goes on to talk about galaxies and black holes and dim stars and red dwarfs and all that moving about in circles, so obedient to the invisible dictates of gravity, aren't we lucky, how without gravity everything would just sink to the bottom, all that celestial debris would pile up down there, just lie there forever, all jumbled up, no place to go, no up—no circles—no parallel universes and all those theoretical speculations—Newton just a laughing stock, Einstein really perplexed, textbooks hopelessly out of touch—powerful telescopes drooping to the ground, airplanes forever grounded, all the ice cream trucks silenced forever, no more ding-a-ling, ding-a-ling, dingle, no more Eskimo bars, rainbows, fifty-fifties, no more Klondikes, not even a small vanilla ice cream in a paper cup with sprinkles.

Colorado

standing at attention
in their trenches
prairie dogs

My Favorite Artist

Were I condemned to live forever on some
desert island, I wouldn't go there without my own
Vermeer, *any* Vermeer—but not the young girl
in the red hat (I would be so far from desire),

rather, something without the provocation, say,
the lady seated at the window, so famously lighted,
the detail. This I would hang on a tree, not too close
to the beach, back about fifty yards, near my hut.

Next, Kline, those sweeping strokes of black and gray
raging on white. This I would put on a post facing
the ocean to scare off intruders, the non-artistic types.
Or, this could serve as a greeting to the aesthetic savior.

Originally created on a garage floor, on a huge canvas
with footprints, tire tracks, what have you, the Pollock
I would take off its frame and spread on the beach
leading from the Kline to the Vermeer.

Finally, the Hopper. Which one? I think *Morning in a City*,
the woman pondering just the right outfit to see her through
the day, maybe even a little lucky. This would go inside
my hut as a reminder of how hard life in the city can be.

Everybody Wants Something Else

I know a lawyer, he wants to be a poet.
I know a poet, he wants to be an engineer.

I know two engineers who want to be artists,
And an airplane pilot who just wants to quit.

I know two sisters who would rather be boys,
And at least one boy who would rather be a girl.

Everybody wants something else,
While gazing all wistful—so unsatisfied—

Over that boring fence in their boring lives,
To where it's all greener, on the other side.

But those who search a greener earth,
More often are greeted with *Astroturf*!

Hard gnarly plastic tough on the feet,
For that restless jumper who had to retreat,

To a spot with palms of a rich green hue,
But the terrible catch is—*you're still just you*!

With the same old dead ends, the same old cramps,
With a little more honey, but the same old ants.

Cheerleader

If I am not for myself, who will be?
If I am only for myself, who am I?
If not now, when?

from the Talmud

It's hard to be your own cheerleader
when you have to get down on the turf
and play ball and would rather stay
up in the bleachers where it's safe,

so no one sees how dumb you look,
fumbling around on the playing field,
the crowd jeering, throwing things—
empty beer bottles, old shoes, folding chairs.

And once you're committed to the fray—
down there on the six-yard line,
the arena jammed with excited spectators
looking down at *you* (poor pigeon),

no one praising your name or looking out for you,
then it's time to think *tactics*—
time to stand tall, start cheering for *you*—
Rah! Rah, Rah! Shish Boom! Bah!

You will look a little strange
jumping up and down,
stabbing the air with your own pom-pom,
shouting your name with gusto—

but then again, they will know enough
to steer clear of you, the crazy one,
that noisy guy waving his arms around,
the one making another touch-down!

68

Why People Are Better Than Dogs

People are better than dogs because they live in big houses
and build big boats and are in charge.
Dogs just do what they are told, sometimes,
and always wear the same clothes.

People can tell other people what to do,
and even make a war on people
to make sure they do the right thing.

Dogs can only fight each other pretty much one on one,
or *canem et canem*, as the saying is, although to be fair
there are dogs way up North somewhere who travel in groups
and can make a bit of trouble.

People in groups and in marriages can sometimes disagree,
but they sometimes work it all out. The only way a dog can
work things out is by looking at you with big brown eyes
and pretending to like you a whole lot, as if we didn't know
it all comes down to that can of Skippy every day.

There was a movie star dog named Lassie and another named
Rin Tin Tin but that was a long time ago and they are the exceptions.

In sum, men have two legs and can wear wing-tip Florsheims,
but dogs have four legs and a tail and have to go barefoot
and just be plain dogs and make the best of it, and that is
to a large extent why we are better than dogs, although
not everyone may agree.

Not the Moon

(fragment found on a scrap of paper)

first side

Not the moon, that crazy slice of seashell, floating, oblivious—
and not the mythical stars, partly extinct long before
their feeble light reaches us, and not the silver tide, swirling about
our retreating footsteps, no, just these hard rocks, old enough,
I believe, to remind me to…cause me to imagine…

other side

Karnac–Roofing–1 gal
Gidden SP 3411
spackle–Dap– Crackshot
joint COMPOUND
roller refills
flashing

70

Art in the Barnyard

Once I tried to write a poem about an albino chicken
        that could have been named *Pierre*
and who wrote poetry, but it didn't work.

Then I tried to write about another chicken, a black bantam
        that painted in the expressionist mode—
á la Franz Kline. No good either.

So I invented a duck inclined to develop artistic *installations*
        of wood and mud—right there
in the barnyard—but who would believe it?

Apparently, some things were just never meant to be,
        let alone a poem about a rooster who made
erotic statues out of balloons and rubber bands,

and fake glass eyeballs, and oversized brassieres,
        or a Cocker Spaniel that...
Well, you see the problem.

Occasionally I think about that white chicken,
        who could have been named *Maurice* or *John Paul*,
and what might become of a poesy of poultry—

querulous chicken quatrains—cocky couplets—
        free-range verse—scratched out,
hatched out—while seeking the birth of a poem?

Marriage between Strangers

People ask me if I think marriage between strangers
should be legal, and I say yes, if it will keep them
off the street, and out of parked cars
at Inspiration Point or the parking lot at Sears.

Marriage should be allowed no matter what the cost.
But it is grievous half the time, and unlucky—
the regal celebration so often erupts into fireworks,
it's a pity god or somebody couldn't be consulted—

let you to stay in that parked car for a while, feel your pulses
more deeply, allow for a change in the weather.

Little Blue Marble

Little blue marble—
amazing image
from outer space.

Not floating on a sea of oatmeal,
or riding on a big fat turtle,
not supported by some sweaty giant
or perched on four enormous pillars—

Just a little blue marble
speeding around
its accomplice, the sun.

How to explain this silly ball
and all the rest—the stars,
the moon, those black holes
with their big appetites?

Not hatched from some rumpy bird,
or whipped up by some restless god—
No, it's just, we're told, one of your everyday
big boomers, just a one-time Ka-Boom!

And there you are—oceans, birds, weeds,
harmonicas, football players, yard sales,
plagues, and lots of wars.

So that's it: Science, which explains everything,
explains nothing, and we are left with a thousand
answers, all beside the question—*Why*?

Oh, mysterious thing of earth, air, foam—
the holy microbe

Ducks

If it looks like a duck,
& quacks like a duck,
& waddles like a duck,
& smells like a duck,
it will *taste* like a duck—

Shoot it!

The Poetry Workshop

Your poem "The Whale in my Back Yard,"
lacks sufficient imagery. I want actually to
hear the sounds of the sea, angry men
in mortal combat—we need a riot of colors,
verbs, adverbs, adjectives, and so forth.

Lose the first eight stanzas—they are really
"just information," anybody can do that.

Great, palpitating, monstrous killer whale
seems rather forced. How about something
simpler, like *big fat whale*?

Tubs of blood coursing down Main St.,
what's that all about? Is blood supposed
to represent the hero's ambivalence toward
whale meat? And what are camels doing in there?

The line breaks lack authority, and you should
never end a line with a double iamb. Here—
lose the last stanza, make the next to last stanza
the first stanza, after the deleted first eight stanzas.

Take out references to the French Revolution,
no one really cares any more. And, just what
does *my callow ex-wife the raging whale killer*
refer to? Can this be made clearer?

You have only one really good stanza,
but we deleted it. Have you read Goethe?

Keeping up with the Macbeths

It's really hard when you live next to the Macbeths,
just impossible beside that big old castle,
with its big private moat, and all those guys
with horns on their heads, and that big pushy wife of his,
the old battle axe—what's her name—
with all the latest furs and stuff, and...oh...that new crown!

They seem to be having the time of their lives over there,
carrying on day and night. And the other night I heard some
terrible sounds over there, sounded like maybe sheep or pigs,
or something being killed—what a god-awful racket!

Of course, I'm jealous, and maybe I'm not being fair. They *do*
have us over for drinks sometimes, especially during the holidays
and they throw really good parties.

Tomorrow I'll think of a reason to just to pop over, say,
to borrow a "cup of mead," why not? See what's happening
with Mac and that awful wife of his, boy, what a temper on that one!

A Panoply of Painters

First was Henri Toulouse Lautrec,
Well-tailored though a physical wreck.
He guzzled the wine,
But his nudes came out fine –
got him into the Louvre by heck!

And then there was Vincent Van Gogh,
Boy, was his credit low!
He cut off an ear
To pay for a beer,
And left for a tip—his big toe!

And then there was Paul Seurat,
Who chose not to wipe but to blot.
His theory was strange:
He tried to arrange
The cosmos by jit and by jot.

And then there was Modigliani.
He never made very much *moni*.
He painted like hell,
But he just couldn't sell.
His models were simply too *scrawny*!

And then there was Salvador Dali,
His work is thought to be jolly,
Oh, there's warp in his wit –
But, look out there, you twit –
A soft watch just slipped off the trolley!

And then there was Pierre A. Renoir,
Who painted with never a *flaw,*
His girls were all dainty,
And looked kind of *fainty,*
Made of ruffles, and icing, and straw.

And don't forget Pablo Picasso,
The Father of Modern Art that's so!
He had periods of blue, and every hue—
He got rich painting any old torso!

And then there was old Franz Kline,
He splashed black and white every time,
You just couldn't tell
Which end was up very well
Till it was hung in a museum sublime.

And don't forget Auguste Rodin,
He had a most clever plan,
He sculpted "The Thinker,"
After many a tinker,
Now everyone *thinks* it's just grand.

And then there was Andy Warhol,
To Campbell's Soup he wafted his *soul,*
He was *très avant garde,*
And he sold by the yard,
But now it's all rather droll.

And who remembers Mr. Kleinholz?
He made dummies that looked like adults.
They screamed and they hollered,
And got everyone bothered,
Now, *who* remembers Mr. Kleinholz?

Poems in Motion

There are poems that, when freshly minted, won't stay still,
keep changing. Overnight, muscular passages sag and lose
their tone;

the next day, held up to the light and shaken, sometimes words
fall out—words that don't belong—even whole phrases like
oh ramshackle stars, rampaging in the firmament…

or *thou maiden, unholy magnet to these rambunctious loins.*
These misadventures are banished quickly, told to
hit the road, jack—take a powder. Vamoose!

Yes, there are poems that change after their inception,
somehow lose their brilliant certitude in the light of
a new day—perfectly good phrases diminish, fall out of grace,

become outsized, overblown, windy, redundant, unwelcome
to the enterprise, and beg for replacement.
How to explain this oddity?

This poem, for example, with its seamless purity,
its airy rigor, only tomorrow will tell if it suffers some loss
of spirit, say, grows wattles under its chin, develops,

mayhap, some odor not sensed earlier.
The motion of poems is something that someone should write about
sometime, spread the news about poems

that change overnight, while the innocent poet,
secure in his Arcadian temple, dreams the dream
of the perfect poem, fit for any god.

Man Stick Dog

I was walking along Dublin Lake in New Hampshire
when I met a small black dog, who greeted me
with bright, staring eyes, and confronted me by looking at me,
then at a stick on the path between us. Repeatedly.

I threw the stick, which was returned in a snap,
and so threw it again. Each time he'd bring it back,
always indicating with his looks from me to the stick
that I had a job to do for him—this little black dog.

This I found endearing, and was reminded of my own lost dog,
the marvelous Achilles, a Saluki, also known as a Gazelle Hound,
and this business with the dog went on for some time.

I was sorely tempted to take the dog with me,
after all, we were good friends now, weren't we?
A synchronous rapport, something very rare, very special.

But then I thought of the owner of the dog.
I looked and saw there was a collar, and presumed a caring
master or mistress must be somewhere near.

I also considered that my new friend might ultimately be unhappy
to be carried off with this new stick thrower—
my only demonstrated value or use.

And so I had to leave one of the best conversations I ever had,
so many years ago, by that small lake—
but oh, what a dialogue we had, all that communication.
Flawless!

Never Give a Sucker an Even Break

Never give a sucker an even break—
but you could buy him a lunch.

Be kind to him, but not too kind.
Talk to him about the folly of his ways,
but the advice will be useless

because we are all suckers anyway,
stuck with being us,

following our own trail,
believing too much, too often,

suckers for the promise of another day—
gift horses, golden elephants,

our very own rainbow
in our very own backyard.

The Great Poet Visits our Class

The great poet entered our room singing,
or humming, gaily. A heavy-set man, he was
all in black—over-sized, baggy shorts, rumpled
shirt, cowboy hat on his hairless dome.

I worried briefly that he might be drunk,
but he quickly dropped a clump of books
on the table and looked about the room
at twenty budding poets.

"So," he said, "how many of you *really want*
to be poets, want it bad enough to walk
over your grandmother's grave to do it?"
One or two hands went up, uncertain.

I thought of my ancient grandmother—
eighty years of cooking and scrubbing,
of Ohio winters, the long trip to California
in 1912, her brothers lost to the "Great War."

So, I said nothing, although…how not
to consider this strange idea? Might one
simple act propel my stalled rhymes
into the gaudy light of publication?

As the hour wore on, my mind wandered
to the resting place of Grandma Rose
and Granddad—and mused:
If this poet's right, I *could* go back

and give a try to graveyard walking—
maybe, even, trample the *two*,
and, what the heck, while at the place,
why not have a go at old Aunt Grace?

82

At the Haiku Convention

Short poets scurry about
Like ants on solitary errands.

Each carries a tiny packet—
A moonbeam here, a cricket there,
Always careful to follow the rules:
one—two—three, *epiphany!*

Things My Daddy Taught Me

Never make fun of a man with a tattoo on his arm
that has a big red heart that says "Mother"
and there's a knife through it dripping bright red blood,
or you played five card stud with and couldn't pay.

Never make fun of another man's wife, car, or dog.
Never borrow another man's car.
Never borrow the car or the wife of a man with a tattoo on his arm.

Never eat in a place called Mom's or Rocky's.
Never eat in a seafood restaurant with a big, fake fish on the roof.
Never eat in a restaurant where you have to kill the fish.
Or the geese. Or the ducks. Or a cow.

Never eat in a restaurant where the drinks have little umbrellas,
the waiters wear sarongs, and everything is flambé. '
Never eat in a place that advertises gumbo.

Never play cards with a man named after a city, a state, or
a prison, like Chicago Charlie, Nevada Smith, or Folsom Freddie.
Never shoot craps with a guy named Snake, or who has a sister
named Sid.

Never make love to girl named Sid with a tattoo on her arm
that says Guido.
Never play cards with a guy named Lucky who is from Vegas or
Chicago. Stay out of Chicago.

Never drink in a place called Harleys End-Of-The-Road
Biker Heaven.
Never make fun of a biker, his dog, his wife—or, most of all—
his bike.
Never argue with a biker whose wife or dog you borrowed.

Never bet on a horse named Fleet Foot, Hurricane, or Lightning.
Never play cards with a horse named Lightning.
Never make fun of a horse with a tattoo that says Mother.

Upon Re-reading Peanuts

Reading Peanuts again, thirty years now,
its creator's progeny still with us, relentless—
I have not managed a similar immortality,

not if you count the heart attack, stroke, ulcers,
as well as lost jobs, lying governments,
teeth that have failed,

but when Lucy entices little Charlie Brown
to try to kick that football as she holds it—
just one more time,

still, I wait in anticipation,
hoping that this time, *this one last time*
he will succeed for all of us,

get the damn thing—but,
as in real life, this elusive goal—
it seems, remains forever ungettable.

Leaving us to soldier on,
waiting for, perhaps, Peanuts III,
sometime later in this beleaguered century

to play one more time, but this time, perhaps,
to have a heart—give Charlie and all of us
a break, kick that thing, something, *anything*!

PART III

A MIND OF WINTER

Night, sleep, death, and stars.

Walt Whitman

After Work at the "Y"

I see him in the local weight room, his body crammed into
black and yellow gym clothes—Adidas, Nike, the "swoosh."

Late in the game for this tired fellow, his face flushed
as he struggles with a tangle of pulleys and weights.

This after a life banging on the great wheel of commerce,
making things go—the hiring and firing, big mergers,

credit card lunches, the Lincoln Town Car—fifty years,
good years probably, pearls for the wife, half-decent schools

for half-decent kids—vacations in sunny places, away from
pressure that never seemed to stop....not too different from

my own travails (and, where'd the time go?) so that now
he has what my doctor calls the "Executive Banana Syndrome,"

one foot on the edge of a golden chute leading right down
to paradise—with me, I'm afraid, not too far behind.

Either way, it's just a matter of time, with the next big decision
to be announced, not by Wall Street, but by the ER—

its blinking lights and dials, its informative gauges—
the thoughtful frown on the doctor's face.

Butterfly

Life is a butterfly, its wings
opening once, only.

Or perhaps a dream
in a secret cove.

Or, and why not, seagulls,
scattered and full of purpose,

until the wings are closed
and the birds silenced,

leaving only poetry
sleeping on white pages.

Jazz Man

A cold, wintry day in Northern New Jersey,
this sign posted on a lone telephone pole:

> *Lost—Black & white mutt,*
> *answers to the name "Jazz Man."*

So, where are you now, *Jazz Man*?
Out on some solo gig—performing for a new,
cool crowd—howling down wild musical nights—
turning on the local *hoi polloi*?

And have you made new friends?
Aficionados who live and breathe jazz,
who can tell the phony from the real,
and really dig your special vibes?

Oh, *Jazz Man,* they are looking for you everywhere,
asking friends, strangers, posting signs—
your doggie bowl is on the back porch, waiting
for you, your toy sax near it, ready for one more set.

Mending

When at last she died,
my grandmother came alive again,
and I could see that stolid figure with needle
and thread, mending my old blue cashmere,
the one with the elbow patches,
complaining all along—
this sweater is too old to mend....

In her time, I expected things to last,
especially those we hold dear,
and counted on her to do whatever
a grandmother ought to do.

She became famous, a family joke,
the night she smuggled forbidden dinner
through my bedroom window—
contraband for an unruly teen.

She was a long time leaving,
gone, in a way, long before the end,
but returned at last to flourish still
in living muscle as it will—to shake
her head again, protest *this sweater
is too old to mend, it's just too old.*

What to Pack When You Go to Heaven

Your best suit, of course, your lucky necktie, two sets
of underwear, warm socks, what else?
Toothbrush, shaving kit—unnecessary,
possibly a few handkerchiefs, linen or silk,
an engraved silver flask for brandy
for those chilly nights there in eternity—
a book of favorite poems, some old love letters
to buoy you up while resting on a fluffy cloud—
perhaps an updated resumé highlighting all
those proud achievements of yours—
marriages, divorces, being hired for that terrific job,
fired from that terrific job—
the promises of love forever under sweeping elms,
and those memories still intact, the beach late in the day
under a mass of wind-swept clouds, the ocean
with its roiling curls, the sand mottled with bits
of seaweed, stretching off so far,
so far into the distance.

In a Word

The soul selects its own society, then shuts the door
—Emily Dickinson

It was not "being understood" that mattered
in and of itself—nor, as the maudlin say—
one soul finding another soul—

but the communion, like all living things,
a mind finding another mind,
reaching into all the corners,

igniting each other,
those private canyons,
no longer a burden,

but coal, now made into living diamond,
allowed at last the miracle of brilliance,
a place to shine.

Afternoon

What have we but questions,
the language of farewell,
and questions always
the questions.

Except
except
the towering ocean,
the palisades,
gulls soaring over the sand.

Regret

Regret, that unwelcome visitor
hanging about all day,
dropping cigarette ashes on the rug,

as relentless as death or taxes.
Only regret goes deeper
and won't let go....

That girl with the pale skin,
the blue of her veins....

The thoughts of might have been.
The dreams of might have been.

About regret I could say
so much, so much more—

but, of course, you already know....

Still, that night the light
casting shadows on her bare skin
as we sank into the darkness....

And the promises,
the promises—
Oh.

Adele

Mine was a mind of winter
this morning—

chill and gray,
until, suddenly
through unexpected portals,
I saw you
shining in the sun.

Atheist

No righteous valley harbors me, no friendly specter tracks
my journey—no entreaties for justice, gold, or other phantoms.

A—without, *theos*—god, a lone tree in the forest,
waiting to fall from that place where no sound comes.

Atheist, not by choice, not by rhyme or rhythm,
simply an accident—one fine day, a shift of thought—

then suddenly abandoned—exiled to a place where
all the signs were new but smudged—where adjustments

had to be made, something to believe in after belief
had been taken away—a new fixity of purpose.

Gone the accustomed multitude, gathering and chanting—
the believers, organized, row on row.

At best a friend to share this world, scrunched down now
into a clarity of vision…shorn of the old entanglements.

Just an old man in a gray suit, all dressed up
with no place to go, all his chips on the black.

Compassion

for Nurse Mary Ann Heller
Jefferson Hospital, Philadelphia, 2009

I had been to the ER and the OR and the hole-in-the-wall gang
had really done a job on me—cauterized a bleeding tongue.

In the movie, *Captain from Castile*, Tyrone Power has a wound.
No doctor about so he and his sidekick drink mucho tequila
and cauterize the wound with a sizzling sword blade, drinking
all the way, hilariously drunk. Hilarious!

But I wasn't laughing. After an hour, my nurse, Mary Ann,
was a fizzled wreck about my indecision whether to go
for more radiation or rest as my surgeon advised.

Exhausted, she started to cry—it was terrible—she was so upset.
I petted her arm, caressed her cheek and we both cried,
so I went to radiation on a gurney, bottles, oxygen and all hanging
on the sides, the craziest thing I ever did and believe me,

with all the tequila in my reckless past, that's saying something.
The next day she came to see how I was and she looked wonderful
and I told her I really liked her hair, and that was true.

Death in the Neighborhood

adapted from a Chinese poem
(translated by E. Pound)

E.R. will rejoice when A.T. is dead—
and A.T. will laugh his fill when
R.A. is finally gone.

And I know, too, that L.N.
down the street,
will be tickled pink
to hear of my demise....

and yet, everyone speaks ill of death!

It's Messy Dying in the Suburbs

All that stuff to be sorted and parceled out
to the grieving, the greedy, the indifferent.

The explanations on engraved stationery,
convergence in a cold, gray building,

organ music tripping the familiar hymns,
the requirement to say something nice.

How much simpler to die in the desert—
one night under scattered stars,

the hills of sand a lucid expanse,
your remains a temporary hummock.

Or there by that pond near that sturdy palm—
that was his favorite spot. His clothes—

worn animal skins—give them to the earth, too,
no need for them now.

100

Miss Ella
Night nurse at the rehab facility

It's midnight and what comes so large, this looming shape,
why, it's Ella, come to save the night, her mellow ministrations.

Once her gentle care is in motion, she hums, something slow,
easy, the tone low and vague, unhurried, which seems to make
everything all OK, at least for another day.

And I know how lucky I am, because I've been Ella-fied,
      mollified,
              satisfied,
                    even perhaps, transmogrified.

And sung to, too,
           these earthy harmonies—

               so rooted in something so right.

Dogwood

See the dogwood—shorn of its summer dress,
so severely bare—what colors will amaze us
when winter relents, apparel landscape with
green surprise—yellow, pink, white—all the colors
the human eye invents, supplies to our amazement
in this bare, uncolored world.

Dove

Mid-March, patches of snow still on the ground,
about one or two in the morning, familiar but
unexpected sounds—three calls in a series, a dove?

A long spondee, a short iamb, then a final, plaintive,
but earnest note—an SOS in the old Morse Code.

And this image, a bird alone in a tree outside
my window as I lie in bed—coooo coo *coooooo*!
Not with a "c," of course, or maybe more like,
arrrruhh, arrrruhh, *arrrruhh*.

Several times I hear these sounds, a bird calling
and waiting, and wonder at the message—a search
for companionship, or simply nature in motion,
the dark outdoors.

I think of the distress, the old disappointments
of waiting for so many things—
and this patient summons on a freezing branch.
Will there be an answer, and would I recognize it?

Fate

When she goes out the door
who knows what fate may have
in store, that simple trip?

What article of grief might
catch my love, crack the plan,
impede her safe return?

The mind invents scenarios
of chance gone wrong, the telephone,
a calm informing voice—

the adventure dropped into a trap,
alas. Or not. But now the news:
At last, she's back!

Music

The first chord is the wonder of it all,
the music for which we have no words.

Searching for them keeps us busy—
whole industries of dead poets.

Is it here?
Is it there?

The clouds taunt us as much as
the stars.

Every tree its own monument
to the mystery.

And then to look within—
the mind exhausts a galaxy of visions.

Its own puzzle inside out.

And always the music,
this dreadful music.

Images—Some Silver, Some Gray

Sketchy thoughts, these—the first day on earth after I die—
that singular first day when I will no longer be here,

but otherwise like any other day—not the place where I have lived
a half century, but another, where the Pacific reliably coats

the shore in silver waves and columns of earth sweep
up from the beach to form looming palisades.

Right by the ocean, my first-remembered home has hardly changed,
and on this day of silver and gray, the sky is streaked with clouds,

clean, fine and twisted. Tropical trees drink in the California sun
while automobiles await their sleeping masters,

and the trees seem not to cast shadows on the ground, but to have
shadows within themselves—I should mention, the leaves

defined by their own shadows—and the branches sit gnarled,
clumped and rugged on their dark, gray trunks.

It is still early morning, no one about yet,
no one in the surf, or walking on the sandy beach.

The world is dreaming without me, without my need,
although…somewhere, a man, regarding the silver gray sky,

contemplates a cigarette, thinks about a time long ago—
as *we* measure time, yes—long ago, and another,

turning in her bed, thinks of me, too…that bright shadow,
in another time...and then, to begin the day,

a small white dog appears, investigates a trash can
on the beach, and somewhere a car starts, sea gulls cry.

106

Jukebox

for Joe Breslin, in memoriam

We all know how the mind is a jukebox, playing its own favorites,
not necessarily nice or good stuff—just depending on the vagaries.
J10 is my 8th grade teacher Miss Pete telling me not to go *pssst!*
to get her attention, since that is a sign of disrespect, at least
in Puerto Rico, a place I'd never been to, so I don't say *pssst!*
any more. K14 is Linda saying, *Oh, never mind,* in that resigned way
she had, speaking volumes I guess. but R19 is Joe Breslin,
with the curt, mocking—*Well, Stanley!* Yes, Laurel & Hardy,
on stage, right here in my head, which is so typical of Joe, always
putting a spin on things, on top of the daily currents that would flow
between us.

Sadly, the real Joe has departed, leaving us an unwelcome, empty
space, and for me, in this new emptiness, some of those things still
keep playing in my head, time to time—silly joke about ice fishing
and keeping worms warm, an occasional exclamation of *doo-dah!*
Doo-dah!, and, of course, that voice that says, over and over,
Well, Stanley, now you've done it!

Meltdown

Perhaps it was inevitable, after three months of constantly offering
to meet a plethora of picky demands—special toothpaste, ointments,
exotic medicines—and one Sunday when I was still able to
stop home for a while, she put on a grim oh so dark face, a face
I hadn't seen since early in our marriage when she put on a hat
scribbled on it, "Don't Talk To Me," and then,
in her consternation, lost her glasses.

No way out, no way to find her driving glasses and she searched
frantically and I searched—where to look, impossible to think—
then I stopped to think more…and went outside and looked
into the back of her black Mercedes, and there, glistening
in the light of a street lamp—*glasses* and *sunglasses*—
which had jumped out of her handbag when thrown in the back
of the car, and there they were, perched on top of her purse.

Triumphant, I ran up the stairs, rang the doorbell as alarm,
shouting *I found them*…and all was well for the day,
but the next day, coming to see me early in the morning,
she ran into a parked truck that was in her path.

She thought it was going to turn, move out of the way, she said.
She called me all jittery and feeling bad and what could I do
but share the sorrow, and tell her it was all right for goodness sake,
and start to look for another little black car.

Men at Sixty

after "Men at Forty" by Donald Justice

Men at sixty,
looking into private mirrors,
study the old warrior bones for signs of wear—
a breaking down of the possible.

They no longer seek that young lifeguard,
find instead the determined swimmer,
champion of small victories.

Men at sixty
remember the ardent father
and those before him—
that long hallway of fathers,
images now running to gray.

They sense the iron vessel of mortality
moving now beneath them,
observe the weather,
so changeable,
look to the North Star—
move forward into the night.

My Father Turns Off the Lights

My father turns off the lights
and room to room I go
faithful to the shadow
the urgency
to save what drains away, day by day
the juice we buy, the time to spend.

Room to room click, click,
no end to it,
saving what I can, a penny here
a penny there

mindful of the need to close the door
preserve the warmth
helpless in the shadow
of my father long ago—

the pennies saved,
click, click,
the shadow on the stair.

Pain

There are no pain receptors for another's pain—
we can only watch the loved one's coughing
and squirm with empathy and commiseration—
all genuine, but within self-contained limits.

We can only watch, help carry the bags,
rearrange the furniture.

Bandages must be worn by others—
but such soulful creatures we are, our arms
extending beyond a single circle or embrace,
into history even—

the Arawaks, the Irish famine, my neighbor across
the street, walking now, but slowly, finding his way
to his front door, dressed against the winter,
determined and alone.

Pavilions

At the age of twenty I lost my belief
in Christianity and its pavilions.

The edifice was, I suppose,
too undermined to survive the many
standing complaints and observations.

The probable final source was an essay
by Einstein, "Out of My Youth,"
in which he made, for me,
the whole apparatus no longer tenable.

And so I dropped through the invisible,
protective template so embraced
by most of my contemporaries here
in the USA and its environs.

But now, let us pray.

Postcard

God is playing tricks with the leaves, they skip
and hop and jump on the green lawn where I look for
the small birds that would explain this leafy agitation,

and I search for the horses—not in view right now—
that would complete this puzzle under the naked trees
that reach skyward, limbs twisted into a pathetic agony

from a gathering at the base, then up and up into spiny forms,
so bereft, so beautiful from my hospital window—
this December postcard on a clear winter day.

Resumé

Son of an alcoholic writer father,
adulterous artist mother,
failed writer brother, a suicide—

Cab driver, sailor, lifeguard, car salesman,
bartender, womanizer—lover of many women,
all abandoned—

Erstwhile pretender, slacker, scant knowledge
of geography, political history, other people's
lives, thoughts, ideas—

Hack writer—maker of instruction manuals,
reports, studies, analyses, unread books,
scattered poems, scribbles upon scribbles—

Did it all, but in small ways—Europe,
Mexico, the pyramids of Egypt, the ruins
of Jamaica—

References: Available, look under
that rock near the front door,
by the broken steps, there where my wife

plants flowers every spring, and birds
search for food—every creature in its turn.

Visitor

I was sitting slumped on my hospital bed
when a visitor came to my window,
a tiny bird mostly a shimmering white
with a pointed yellow beak, and it looked
toward me, inquisitive I thought, and so cold
outside this winter morning, it seemed to look
about, want to come in, and I had to wish it could,
maybe have some crumbs for breakfast
away from the cold, share ideas and what's going
on around town, no politics, of course, just small
talk, keep off the chill outside, be together.

Rhetorical Questions

What if I wrote a poem and no one read it?
What if I went to heaven and no one was there?
What if I wanted to swim and couldn't find an ocean?
And what if I loved you and you weren't here—
How could I begin again?

After Cancer

I found this house
I found this woman
I hammered this nail

and now, adrift on
circadian rhythms

once more, try to gather
the reason, the reasons

to lift this winter afternoon
higher
as far as one might go—

above thought
above the snow-scattered field
beyond the mind's horizon

to search a new vision—
so hard to see
so obscure.

This Ocean, This Sea

In this sea of troubles no man knows
where he will be buried, what winds

will favor his path, its track.
The best hope, a length of days

and grace in the going, or if not that,
a good friend, at least that bounty,

a hand outreaching, a reason for peace,
any reason.

Missing Mansour

We went to job fairs together, looking for work.
One of us was black, I'm not sure which.

He was named Mansour—the same as a city or district
in the Near East, a name I have noticed in the news
surrounding our misadventures there.

We became acquainted at RCA, one of the most famous
names in American industry—which was taken over and
absorbed by an even bigger company while we were there.

At the job fairs we wore suits and ties designed to prove
we were still worth something, and got some nifty stuff,
like canvas bags and our social security cards laminated.

Mansour hated meetings, he said, and had a wonderful
laugh that I wrote a poem about—how it would escalate up,
a rich ringing pitch, then climb down slowly and fade,
mellifluous.

A phone call the other day ended our friendship,
and I've been trying to think what to say about it ever since,
to write the lovely lady left behind by a stealthy heart
that turned treacherous one night, left us Mansourless,
a new kind of poverty we must endure.

What is the Age Appropriate?

What is the age appropriate
to give up, resign
to read the writing as it is writ

to see it canceled
every line?

What is the age
when sleep will gain
enough to close the mind
its never stopping quest

the fact of air suffice
the very fact of it
the enterprise

this broken thing
this whirl of dust
this here and now and must?

My Will

To my wife, I leave my abiding spirit,
my sense of humor, my hits and misses,
rights and wrongs, my good intentions,
my lust for all things carnal—your arms, legs,
teeth—your wonderfully small ears,
your face which aged and didn't age
over thirty years, your wrenching laughter
that brought the daylight in—the memories
of nights so dark we could not hide
but struggled on as many do.

Who, with me, persisted on the money trail,
selling our lives by the hour
for *services rendered*, giving what we could
to each other, to friends…modest luxuries,
the little we could manage.

As for those who crossed my way but briefly
whose finest compliment was the back leaning…
what a character ?…to those, so content within
their own margins never to create something
from nothing, which is to say, to tinker with
the stuff of art—to these I say *pfhhht*!

But to those I could find to love, fellow visitors
to this wondrous enterprise—to that small armada,
I will my thanks and regret for any harm that I did do
and was unable to undo, especially to those who loved
me unguardedly, subject to my ungainly need.

To this vanishing world, then, this final note—
there was a space of time when I was loved, and loved
a few, just as so many have been known to do.

Judgment

I stood before the tall, gaunt figure.
His dead gray eyes were like weathered granite,
and, as he regarded me, a frown seemed to play
on his ashen face.

After some deliberation,
he produced a large, black book
and placed it on a small table between us.

With a brief sigh, he opened the book,
and after a quick search found a place.
He stopped to look at me, then ran a gnarled,
faintly yellow finger down one page,
pausing at times to slow his scrutiny,
and apparently weigh whatever
was in the mysterious book.

He continued to the bottom,
where a faint light seemed to appear.
Turning to the next page, a somewhat darker color
seemed to settle near the book, and he moved
down the page, once more, stopping here and there.

After some silence, the book was closed,
and I was asked if I had any questions.

Didn't I have a question? he said,
there are always questions...

I replied that I did,
but couldn't think what it was.

Saying Farewell

It was not a good time to die—ten more payments due
on the Mercedes, and the house still not done after thirty
years—the unfinished room with the bar in the basement,
the alleged lounge—the new lawn not yet taken hold.

And my wife—without me, the things she'll never get right—
the stereo with its bizarre Chinese programming,
the chandelier that only takes a special kind of bulb,
the exact location of the insurance papers—what else?

But there he was, I could see him through the kitchen window,
coming up the back stairs, as if he knows his proper place,
perhaps weary of the alarm he spreads when there are
too many about, the sudden silence, the stricken looks.

The day had started nicely enough, backache not too bad
once I got going. And the newspaper delivered at last,
after all the hassle with the new paperboy—yes, things
were looking pretty good, snow about gone.

As he approached the back door, I thought to open it,
save him the trouble, be friendly, who knows, he might
change his mind—on a whim, say? Perhaps a small
postponement, time to get things in order.

At the top of the stairs, the dark figure hesitated,
seeming to me terribly burdened, as if trailing some
great sadness, and appeared to have trouble moving,
so I thought to make this easy—not add to his distress.

I asked him in, offered him a drink—tomato juice?
Hot chocolate? I inquired about his trip, but at this
He seemed to bristle, so I asked if I might just turn out
The lights, perhaps lock the back door—leave a small note?

Thirteen Ways to Make an Exit

Tell your spouse you're going out for cigarettes,
Will be back in a minute.
Take nothing with you, no extra clothes,
No toothpaste—just start driving,
Drive until everything you know is behind you
And you are on your way to new,
Undiscovered roads, through a vast, green valley
Leading into smoke-colored mountains—
Just see how far you can go, yes,
How far you can go,
See…how you can go…now…*go*!

II
When entering buildings, fail to locate all the Exit signs,
Those bright red Exit Signs put there to promote escape,
To keep you from harm, the incipient harm—
The ever present potential of harm—in case of fire
You must exit. Oh, just Exit. *Exeunt all*!

III
Languish on yet another battlefield,
Wearing yet another uniform, replete with epaulets,
Brass buttons, Sam Brown belt…
Scabbard, cutlass, foil, mace and hammer…
Good Conduct Medal.

IV
Turn left when you were supposed to turn right.
The others got it right, why didn't you?
At the light, what light?
That light, right there, always turn right,
Everything depends on it:
Everything! Right?

V
Hack something out of the earth,
An inheritance for some—hacking coal, hacking silver—
Hacking stuff for money, money and stuff,
Hacking through gas and dust and gas.
Gas—dangerous stuff, gas!

VI
Uncork a bottle of bubbly—
(The real thing, all the way from France!)
Celebrate your good fortune,
That awesome deal, celebrate a lot!
Mud in your eye, Happy Days!
Drink a little too much, or a lot too much.
When the party's over,
Send everyone away, then slip on shiny
Hardwood floors, bleeding…alone…so alone…
Next week, it's in all the papers. *Cheers!*

VII
Under the knife, trust complete strangers
To fix something terribly wrong—
Fix something terribly wrong,
Strangers with remarkable skills…still…

VIII
Take a trip, a vacation, why not?
On the new trans-oceanic cattle car,
Trans-earth, trans-sky, trans-everything,
Truly a Chariot of Fire, enough to turn Apollo bright green!
The one that's unsinkable—yes, that's the one:
Unsinkable!

IX
Run from your fellow inmates
Who thought you meant to harm them,
Your fellow prisoners, inmates, good colleagues all
But somehow a mistake,
No way to fix it now, unfixable. Run!

X
In your four-poster bed,
The one with fake pineapples,
Surrounded by friends and heirs,

A bishop or two, jugglers, acrobats—
Possibly the court jester (an amiable dwarf).—
Observe this dank chorus of loss.
Note, too, how on the horizon, dark clouds gather,
A sign of grisly weather—perhaps a blight on the crops,
The entire nation gone to mourning—
Icing on the cake

XI
Swim out to sea, mindless of direction,
Mindless of purpose,
Working simply against the tide,
The relentless tide, relentless…the tide…
Swimming, swimming, swimming…the tide…

XII
Open the window. You need fresh air.
Try to remember those years at the beach,
The beautiful girls dressed in colorful scraps—
Try to push away the black cloud,
That enormous black cloud that's always there, won't go away—
That's it, open the window, you just need *fresh air*—
You can do it, now fly, fly…*fly away*!

XIII
Hot air balloon!

About the Author

John was born April 12, 1933, in Santa Monica, California, to Margaret Payne Bourne, an artist, and Setliffe Hunter Bourne, a journalist. Since his father worked for The United Press and was transferred from bureau to bureau, John spent his childhood moving about the Northwest, but returned every summer to his grandparents' home in Santa Monica. From the time John was five, his grandfather, a precision engineer at Northrop, helped him build road-worthy soapbox derby cars.

If John wanted something he was expected to work for it. This led to a wide range of experiences and the confidence to accept successively steeper challenges. At nine, his first job was gathering walnuts on an Oregon farm for 35 cents an hour. Thus he could buy model kits of WWII planes which he built, hung in his room, and then made paintings of as if they were in action. These blurry watercolors his mother saved for fifty years.

In the seventh grade, tired of being the new kid—six schools in six years—he refused to move again. The family returned to Santa Monica. His father left journalism to become a press agent and comedy writer and his mother worked as art director for the nascent CBS-TV station.

An Eagle Scout at 14, John learned a lot about birds and survived survival camp. His multiple paper routes forced him to get up every morning at 4 a.m. but also allowed him, two years before he could legally drive, to buy a '25 Ford. He hid it in a neighbor's garage. When it was discovered, his mother helped him paint it chartreuse.

High school, found him, as his notes say, with a "Cool convertible, hi- stack manifold, lowered, fender skirts, dual muffler / Me in duck-tails, cruising around Bell High School (trouble), dancing the New Yorker." He was also an honor student, a varsity swimmer, captain of the debate team, a member of the World Federalists, and president of the student body.

During the summer between high school and college, this champion debater became top salesman on a used car lot, but quit when he found people were buying cars, they couldn't afford. As a lifeguard he taught 300 kids to swim.

While at UCLA, songwriting, a girl with perfect pitch, and war in Korea derailed John's plans to become a lawyer. He joined the Coast Guard Reserve, played the tuba in the Coast Guard band, and was called up in 1953. After basic training he was sent to Radioman School in Groton, Connecticut, and served as Radioman Petty Officer aboard the USCGC *Evergreen* on iceberg duty in the North Atlantic as well as on search and rescue out of New Bedford on USCGC *Yakutat*. Released from active duty in 1955, he tended bar on Cape Cod, drove a cab in Boston, and returned to UCLA in 1956 on the GI Bill.

John majored in philosophy, while studying nearly everything else, and supporting himself with his usual array of unusual part-time jobs. Honorably discharged from the Coast Guard Reserve in l960, he received his BA in 1962. By this time, he had taken a job as a technical writer. Soon, with top secret clearance, he was working as a human factors analyst and consultant in computer-based-training on projects for the U.S. air defense system, for NASA, and for various companies around the country.

In 1960, John had married Ingeborg Düssler-Düring, an actress and artist who had studied at the Munich Conservatory of Fine Arts. She was a survivor—more or less—of the Dresden bombing. John, to his great sorrow, found with Inge there were problems that he could not solve. They were divorced in l964. During the next eight years, along with "seriously non-serial dating," John spent his weekends painting and sculpting, sharing a studio with the artist Gloria Burton, who taught him welding. He sold his work at street fairs, later placed some in galleries, won some prizes, and took intensive courses in photography.

By 1969, military contracts had dried up and the company he worked for was struggling so he became an independent consultant. In 1972 he accepted a job at an insurance company in Philadelphia. On the day he was to leave for the East Coast, his younger brother died.

John found a house in New Hope, PA, commuted to Philadelphia during the week and to New York on weekends. His former roommate from Laurel Canyon days—who was one of my oldest friends—invited John to a barbeque on Long Island where our mutual friend and his wife wanted John and me to meet. That I was a divorced school teacher with three children and a complicated life and background did not scare John off. A year later, we married and moved to Moorestown, NJ.

As the children were growing up, John applied problem-solving techniques: "Confrontation, negotiation, conciliation, celebration!" There *were* celebrations—recitals, concerts, plays, soccer, hockey and lacrosse games, birthdays, anniversaries, holidays, engagements, weddings, christenings, vacations in New Hampshire, Cape Cod, Colorado and California—the happiest of times. And John stood by me in the blackest of times. In 1987, our youngest was lost to us.

John also cared for his parents, who drove across country to live with us in 1980, and then moved to a home nearby. His father, "Nick," at 78 still did work for a few clients. His mother, "Peggy," came home after chemotherapy sessions to plant a garden, refinish an old chest, or make a quilt. She died in 1983; Nick ten years later, John by his side.

Meanwhile, through designing training systems for diverse clients from dry cleaning establishments to automatic railroad systems, with long commutes, frequent travel, tight deadlines, and difficult challenges, John provided for us all. Between assignments, there was time for family, poetry, humor books, photography, and sailing on Barnegat Bay or the Delaware. But just when a manuscript of his poems was ready to send out, another challenge came along.

In 2001, cancer forced John to retire completely. In remission until 2009, he used this unexpected sabbatical to concentrate on poetry by taking writing courses, participating in poetry groups, giving readings, winning some prizes, publishing in various journals, and always sharing these adventures with me.

W. H. Auden wrote, "...there is only one thing all poetry must do; it must praise all it can for being and for happening...." John would agree. This sketch cannot do him justice, but his poems can. I have found in his poems a healing joy, and hope others will, too.

Adele M. Bourne